This Baby Book: The First 5 Years

Is Dedicated To:

_____

DEDICATION

This book is dedicated to all the new parents out there.

You are my inspiration in producing baby books especially to record keepsake memories that will last a lifetime.

ow To Use This Baby Book; The First Five Years Keepsake Log Book:

s ultimate baby book the first five years notebook is a perfect way to track and record all your
w baby memories. This unique baby's book: the first 5 years notebook is a great way to keep all of
ur keepsake information all in one place.

ch interior page includes prompts and space to record the following:

1. Great Expectations - Write the memories of the baby's arrival in the journal notes.

2. Welcome To The World - Record the baby's arrival and important memories of that day. And
    the first five years as well.

3. Dear Baby - Construct your love letter and the heart feels you'd like to share..upon birth and
    through the first five years. so as to be reminded later when reminiscing...

4. Baby's First through 5th Year - Record funny, silly and important events about the baby's first
    through the 5th year.

5. Take a photo, record your thoughts - Stay on task using this photo page to insert your favorite
    picture of your baby from ages 1 -5. Special memories can be written right on the page.

6. Birthday Page - Space to put a yearly picture of the baby while celebrating the birthday
    milestones.

7. Monthly Progress Report - Record milestones of baby's first through the 5th year.

8. Note Pages - For more journaling and thoughts on baby's growth. Write out all the heartfelt
    memories of love for your new baby.

9. Say Cheese - baby's tooth page, so to keep track of when the teething begins.

10. Family Tree - Record on both sides of the family, so the baby can trace family lineage.

ave Fun!

BABY BOOK
The first 5 years
— GREAT EXPECTATIONS —

BABY BOOK
The first 5 years
— GREAT EXPECTATIONS —

_____

_____

_____

_____

_____

_____

_____

_____

_____

_____

_____

_____

_____

_____

_____

_____

_____

_____

_____

BABY BOOK
The first 5 years
— GREAT EXPECTATIONS —

BABY BOOK
The first 5 years
—WELCOME TO THE WORLD—

_____

_____

_____

_____

_____

_____

_____

_____

_____

_____

_____

_____

_____

_____

_____

_____

_____

_____

_____

_____

BABY BOOK
The first 5 years
—WELCOME TO THE WORLD—

BABY BOOK
The first 5 years
—WELCOME TO THE WORLD—

BABY BOOK
The first 5 years
—DEAR BABY—

_____

_____

_____

_____

_____

_____

_____

_____

_____

_____

_____

_____

_____

_____

_____

_____

_____

_____

BABY BOOK
The first 5 years
—DEAR BABY—

_____

_____

_____

_____

_____

_____

_____

_____

_____

_____

_____

_____

_____

_____

_____

_____

_____

_____

_____

BABY BOOK
The first 5 years
—DEAR BABY—

BABY BOOK
The first 5 years
—ALL ABOUT BABY—

_____

_____

_____

_____

_____

_____

_____

_____

_____

_____

_____

_____

_____

_____

_____

_____

_____

_____

_____

_____

_____

BABY BOOK
The first 5 years
—ALL ABOUT BABY—

_____

_____

_____

_____

_____

_____

_____

_____

_____

_____

_____

_____

_____

_____

_____

_____

BABY BOOK
The first 5 years
—ALL ABOUT BABY—

BABY BOOK
The first 5 years
—BABYS FIRST YEAR—

BABY BOOK
The first 5 years
—BABYS FIRST YEAR—

_____

_____

_____

_____

_____

_____

_____

_____

_____

_____

_____

_____

_____

_____

_____

_____

_____

_____

_____

_____

BABY BOOK
The first 5 years
_ SAVE YOUR PHOTOS AND _
RECORD YOUR THOUGHTS

From the moment you hear the good news through Baby's fifth birthday party!

BABY BOOK
The first 5 years
—BIRTHDAY PAGE—

BABY BOOK
The first 5 years
—MONTHLY PROGRESS—

_____
_____
_____
_____
_____
_____
_____
_____
_____
_____
_____
_____
_____
_____
_____
_____
_____
_____
_____
_____
_____
_____
_____
_____

BABY BOOK
The first 5 years
—MONTHLY PROGRESS—

_____

_____

_____

_____

_____

_____

_____

_____

_____

_____

_____

_____

_____

_____

_____

_____

_____

_____

_____

_____

_____

_____

_____

BABY BOOK
The first 5 years
—MONTHLY PROGRESS—

BABY BOOK
The first 5 years
— NOTES —

BABY BOOK
The first 5 years
— NOTES —

_____

_____

_____

_____

_____

_____

_____

_____

_____

_____

_____

_____

_____

_____

_____

_____

_____

_____

BABY BOOK
The first 5 years
— NOTES —

BABY BOOK
The first 5 years
— NOTES —

BABY BOOK
The first 5 years
— NOTES —

_____

_____

_____

_____

_____

_____

_____

_____

_____

_____

_____

_____

_____

_____

_____

_____

_____

_____

_____

BABY BOOK
The first 5 years
—ONE TO TWO YEARS OLD—

BABY BOOK
The first 5 years
—ONE TO TWO YEARS OLD—

BABY BOOK
The first 5 years
_ SAVE YOUR PHOTOS AND _
RECORD YOUR THOUGHTS ‾

From the moment you hear the good news through Baby's fifth birthday party!

BABY BOOK
The first 5 years
—BIRTHDAY PAGE—

_____

_____

_____

_____

_____

_____

_____

_____

BABY BOOK
The first 5 years
—MONTHLY PROGRESS—

_____
_____
_____
_____
_____
_____
_____
_____
_____
_____
_____
_____
_____
_____
_____
_____
_____
_____
_____
_____
_____
_____
_____

BABY BOOK
The first 5 years
—MONTHLY PROGRESS—

BABY BOOK
The first 5 years
—MONTHLY PROGRESS—

_____
_____
_____
_____
_____
_____
_____
_____
_____
_____
_____
_____
_____
_____
_____
_____
_____
_____
_____
_____
_____
_____

BABY BOOK
The first 5 years
— NOTES —

BABY BOOK
The first 5 years
—NOTES—

BABY BOOK
The first 5 years
— NOTES —

BABY BOOK
The first 5 years
— NOTES —

_____

_____

_____

_____

_____

_____

_____

_____

_____

_____

_____

_____

_____

_____

_____

_____

_____

_____

BABY BOOK
The first 5 years
— NOTES —

BABY BOOK
The first 5 years
—TWO TO THREE YEARS OLD—

_____

_____

_____

_____

_____

_____

_____

_____

_____

_____

_____

_____

_____

_____

_____

_____

_____

_____

BABY BOOK
The first 5 years
—TWO TO THREE YEARS OLD—

BABY BOOK
The first 5 years

SAVE YOUR PHOTOS AND
RECORD YOUR THOUGHTS

From the moment you hear the good news through Baby's fifth birthday party!

BABY BOOK
The first 5 years
—BIRTHDAY PAGE—

_____
_____
_____
_____
_____
_____
_____

BABY BOOK
The first 5 years
—MONTHLY PROGRESS—

BABY BOOK
The first 5 years
—MONTHLY PROGRESS—

BABY BOOK
The first 5 years
—MONTHLY PROGRESS—

BABY BOOK
The first 5 years
— NOTES —

_____

_____

_____

_____

_____

_____

_____

_____

_____

_____

_____

_____

_____

_____

_____

_____

_____

_____

_____

_____

_____

BABY BOOK
The first 5 years
— NOTES —

_____

_____

_____

_____

_____

_____

_____

_____

_____

_____

_____

_____

_____

_____

_____

_____

BABY BOOK
The first 5 years
— NOTES —

BABY BOOK
The first 5 years
— NOTES —

BABY BOOK
The first 5 years
— NOTES —

BABY BOOK
The first 5 years
—THREE TO FOUR YEARS OLD—

BABY BOOK
The first 5 years
—THREE TO FOUR YEARS OLD—

_____

_____

_____

_____

_____

_____

_____

_____

_____

_____

_____

_____

_____

_____

_____

_____

_____

_____

_____

_____

_____

_____

_____

BABY BOOK
The first 5 years
_ SAVE YOUR PHOTOS AND _
RECORD YOUR THOUGHTS

From the moment you hear the good news through Baby's fifth birthday party!

_____

_____

_____

_____

_____

_____

BABY BOOK
The first 5 years
—BIRTHDAY PAGE—

_____

_____

_____

_____

_____

_____

_____

_____

BABY BOOK
The first 5 years
—MONTHLY PROGRESS—

_____
_____
_____
_____
_____
_____
_____
_____
_____
_____
_____
_____
_____
_____
_____
_____
_____
_____
_____
_____
_____
_____
_____
_____
_____

BABY BOOK
The first 5 years
—MONTHLY PROGRESS—

BABY BOOK
The first 5 years
—MONTHLY PROGRESS—

_____
_____
_____
_____
_____
_____
_____
_____
_____
_____
_____
_____
_____
_____
_____
_____
_____
_____
_____
_____
_____
_____
_____
_____

BABY BOOK
The first 5 years
— NOTES —

BABY BOOK
The first 5 years
— NOTES —

_____

_____

_____

_____

_____

_____

_____

_____

_____

_____

_____

_____

_____

_____

_____

_____

_____

BABY BOOK
The first 5 years
—NOTES—

BABY BOOK
The first 5 years
— NOTES —

_____

_____

_____

_____

_____

_____

_____

_____

_____

_____

_____

_____

_____

_____

_____

_____

_____

_____

_____

_____

BABY BOOK
The first 5 years
— NOTES —

BABY BOOK
The first 5 years
—FOUR TO FIVE YEARS OLD—

_____

_____

_____

_____

_____

_____

_____

_____

_____

_____

_____

_____

_____

_____

_____

_____

_____

BABY BOOK
The first 5 years
—FOUR TO FIVE YEARS OLD—

BABY BOOK
The first 5 years
_ SAVE YOUR PHOTOS AND _
RECORD YOUR THOUGHTS

From the moment you hear the good news through Baby's fifth birthday party!

_____

_____

_____

_____

_____

_____

BABY BOOK
The first 5 years
—BIRTHDAY PAGE—

BABY BOOK
The first 5 years
—MONTHLY PROGRESS—

_____
_____
_____
_____
_____
_____
_____
_____
_____
_____
_____
_____
_____
_____
_____
_____
_____
_____
_____
_____
_____
_____
_____
_____

BABY BOOK
The first 5 years
—MONTHLY PROGRESS—

BABY BOOK
The first 5 years
—MONTHLY PROGRESS—

_____

_____

_____

_____

_____

_____

_____

_____

_____

_____

_____

_____

_____

_____

_____

_____

_____

_____

_____

_____

_____

_____

_____

BABY BOOK
The first 5 years
— NOTES —

BABY BOOK
The first 5 years
— NOTES —

_____

_____

_____

_____

_____

_____

_____

_____

_____

_____

_____

_____

_____

_____

_____

_____

_____

_____

BABY BOOK
The first 5 years
— NOTES —

BABY BOOK
The first 5 years
— NOTES —

BABY BOOK
The first 5 years
— NOTES —

_____

_____

_____

_____

_____

_____

_____

_____

_____

_____

_____

_____

_____

_____

_____

_____

_____

_____

_____

_____

_____

BABY BOOK
The first 5 years
— BEYOND FIVE YEARS OLD —

_____

_____

_____

_____

_____

_____

_____

_____

_____

_____

_____

_____

_____

_____

_____

_____

BABY BOOK
The first 5 years
— BEYOND FIVE YEARS OLD —

BABY BOOK
The first 5 years
— BEYOND FIVE YEARS OLD —

BABY BOOK
The first 5 years
— BEYOND FIVE YEARS OLD —

_____

_____

_____

_____

_____

_____

_____

_____

_____

_____

_____

_____

_____

_____

_____

_____

_____

_____

_____

_____

_____

BABY BOOK
The first 5 years
— BEYOND FIVE YEARS OLD —

_____
_____
_____
_____
_____
_____
_____
_____
_____
_____
_____
_____
_____
_____
_____
_____
_____
_____
_____
_____
_____

BABY BOOK
The first 5 years
_ SAVE YOUR PHOTOS AND _
RECORD YOUR THOUGHTS

om the moment you hear the good news through Baby's fifth birthday party!

_____

_____

_____

_____

_____

_____

_____

_____

BABY BOOK
The first 5 years
—BIRTHDAY PAGE—

_____
_____
_____
_____
_____
_____

BABY BOOK
The first 5 years
—MONTHLY PROGRESS—

BABY BOOK
The first 5 years
—MONTHLY PROGRESS—

_____
_____
_____
_____
_____
_____
_____
_____
_____
_____
_____
_____
_____
_____
_____
_____
_____
_____
_____
_____
_____
_____
_____

BABY BOOK
The first 5 years
—MONTHLY PROGRESS—

_____
_____
_____
_____
_____
_____
_____
_____
_____
_____
_____
_____
_____
_____
_____
_____
_____
_____
_____
_____
_____
_____
_____
_____
_____
_____
_____
_____
_____
_____
_____
_____

BABY BOOK
The first 5 years
— NOTES —

BABY BOOK
The first 5 years
— NOTES —

BABY BOOK
The first 5 years
— NOTES —

BABY BOOK
The first 5 years
— NOTES —

BABY BOOK
The first 5 years
— NOTES —

BABY BOOK
The first 5 years
— MILESTONE & ACHIEVEMENTS —

ilestone	Date

te about an event ...

ipped...

d shoes...

e how, why and when questions...

uld recite own street and town...

uld string small beads...

uld catch a ball easily

by's other milestones and highlights...

BABY BOOK
The first 5 years
—SPECIAL DAYS—

_____

_____

_____

_____

_____

_____

_____

_____

_____

_____

_____

_____

_____

_____

_____

_____

BABY BOOK
The first 5 years
—OUR GROWING FAMILY—

BABY BOOK
The first 5 years
— NOTES —

_____

_____

_____

_____

_____

_____

_____

_____

_____

_____

_____

_____

_____

_____

_____

_____

_____

_____

BABY BOOK
The first 5 years
—OUR GROWING FAMILY—

BABY BOOK
The first 5 years
— NOTES —

_____

_____

_____

_____

_____

_____

_____

_____

_____

_____

_____

_____

_____

_____

_____

_____

_____

_____

BABY BOOK
The first 5 years
—OUR GROWING FAMILY—

BABY BOOK
The first 5 years
— NOTES —

_____

_____

_____

_____

_____

_____

_____

_____

_____

_____

_____

_____

_____

_____

_____

_____

_____

BABY BOOK
The first 5 years
—OUR GROWING FAMILY—

BABY BOOK
The first 5 years
— NOTES —

_____

_____

_____

_____

_____

_____

_____

_____

_____

_____

_____

_____

_____

_____

_____

BABY BOOK
The first 5 years
—OUR GROWING FAMILY—

BABY BOOK
The first 5 years
—FAMILY TREE—

GREAT-GRANDMOTHER
_____
Name
_____
Birth date & place

GREAT-GRANDMOTHER
_____
Name
_____
Birth date & place

GREAT-GRANDFATHER
_____
Name
_____
Birth date & place

GREAT-GRANDFATHER
_____
Name
_____
Birth date & place

GREAT-GRANDMOTHER
_____
Name
_____
Birth date & place

GREAT-GRANDMOTHER
_____
Name
_____
Birth date & place

GREAT-GRANDFATHER
_____
Name
_____
Birth date & place

GREAT-GRANDFATHER
_____
Name
_____
Birth date & place

MATERNAL GRANDMOTHER
_____
Name
_____
Birth date & place

PATERNAL GRANDMOTHER
_____
Name
_____
Birth date & place

MATERNAL GRANDFATHER
_____
Name
_____
Birth date & place

PATERNAL GRANDFATHE
_____
Name
_____
Birth date & place

MOTHER
_____
Name
_____
Birth date & place

FATHER
_____
Name
_____
Birth date & place

BABY!
_____
Name

BABY BOOK
The first 5 years
— NOTES —

BABY BOOK
The first 5 years
—SAY CHEESE—

Baby began teething at ....

Baby's first tooth appeared at ....

How Baby fared with teething ....

Teething remedies ....

WHEN BABY'S TEETH APPEARED
(Write dates on tooth images.)

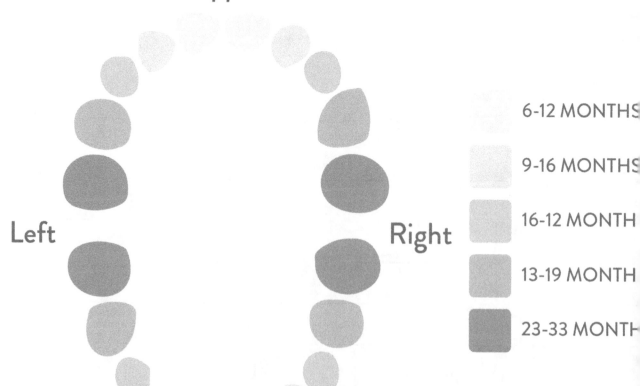

Upper

Left

Right

Lower

6-12 MONTHS

9-16 MONTHS

16-12 MONTH

13-19 MONTH

23-33 MONTH

BABY BOOK
The first 5 years
— NOTES —

BABY BOOK
The first 5 years
— NOTES —

BABY BOOK
The first 5 years
— NOTES —

BABY BOOK
The first 5 years
— NOTES —

_____

_____

_____

_____

_____

_____

_____

_____

_____

_____

_____

_____

_____

_____

_____

_____

_____

BABY BOOK
The first 5 years
— NOTES —

BABY BOOK
The first 5 years
— NOTES —

Printed in the USA
CPSIA information can be obtained
at www.ICGtesting.com
LVHW081544131223
766418LV00013B/333

9 781649 3024